TABLE OF (

➤●◄

Unless otherwise indicated, all Scripture quotations are taken from the King James Version of the Bible.
Seeds Of Wisdom On The Word Of God
ISBN 1-56394-111-2/B-117
Copyright © 2001 by **MIKE MURDOCK**
All publishing rights belong exclusively to Wisdom International.
Published by The Wisdom Center • 4051 Denton Hwy. • Ft. Worth, TX 76117
1-888-WISDOM-1 (1-888-947-3661) • **Website: thewisdomcenter.tv**

WHY I WROTE THIS BOOK.

My Greatest Mind Battle Was Over The Word.
When I entered my late teens, intense warfare emerged in my mind. It seemed that contradictions in the Scriptures existed. Then, I began to doubt the validity of the Bible when I saw hypocrisy in believers, inconsistencies in ministers and my own difficulty to live "the Biblical standard."

Two years of erratic and emotional turmoil occurred. I loved the presence of God and *received* from the Word of God. However, it seemed that the *logic* of my mind and the *faith* in my heart were in constant opposition. One day in honest desperation I asked the Lord to provide confidence and inner peace that the Bible was truly His infallible Word, not merely the compilation of human thoughts and ideas.

Three powerful truths emerged:

1. No Human Would Have Written A Standard As High As The Scriptures Teach. No husband would have written to treat your wife like Christ treats the church. No wife would have written to obey your husband. No teenager would have written that foolishness is bound in the heart of a child, but the rod of correction will drive it far from him. No rich man would have admitted that he that trusts in his riches will fail.

2. The Changes That Occur In Those Who Embrace The Word Of God Are Supernatural. Drug addiction has been broken. Alcoholics have been set free and delivered. Those who are violent have become meek and submissive.

3. The Very Presence Of A Bible Often Produces An Aura And Change In The Atmosphere. I have been on planes and noted an entire group of people become instantly silent when I pulled out my Bible. No novel of fiction affects men like this. Encyclopedias do not affect men like this. Lay a dictionary on a restaurant table. Nobody looks at you twice. But, lay a Bible on a restaurant table in visible view, and they will stare at you the entire meal. The magnetism of the Word of God is indescribable, irrefutable and unforgettable.

Yet, it is the Unused Weapon, the Undiscovered Map, the Untapped Well of Wisdom on earth. It is the Master Weapon provided to us by the Father to escape satanic deception and snares.

The Gospel contains two Forces:

1. The *Person* of Christ.
2. The *Principles* of Christ.

The *Person* of Jesus creates your *peace*.
The *Principles* create your *prosperity*.
The *Person* of Jesus prepares you for *Eternity*.
The *Principles* prepare you for *Earth*.

The Word Of God Will Solve Every Problem In Your Life.

That's why I wrote this book.

Mike Murdock

God's Only Pain
    Is To Be *Doubted.*
God's Only Pleasure
    Is To Be *Believed.*

-MIKE MURDOCK

≈ 1 ≈

THE WORD OF GOD IS THE MOST IMPORTANT BOOK ON EARTH.

The Word Of God Is Your Success Handbook.
Encyclopedias impart knowledge of people, places and events. Dictionaries impart knowledge of words. But, nothing is as important as the Wisdom of God for communicating Laws of Success for your life.

11 Reasons Why The Bible Is The Most Important Book On Earth

1. The Word Of God Is The Wisdom Of God. What is Wisdom? Wisdom is simply the Law of God applied accurately to solve your problem. Wisdom is the *scriptural solution* to any problem you are facing. "For this is your Wisdom and your understanding" (Deuteronomy 4:6; see also 2 Peter 3:15, Proverbs 2:6).

2. The Word Of God Is The Love Book Of The Universe. The Word explains the love of God. "For God so loved the world, that He gave His only begotten Son, that whosoever believeth in Him should not perish, but have everlasting life" (John 3:16; see also 1 John 3:16, 1 John 4:8, Jude 21).

3. The Word Of God Is A Book On Order.
Order Is The Accurate Arrangement Of Things (see 1 Chronicles 12:33). It shows the rewards of honoring authority, parental authority and even spiritual authority.

4. The Word Of God Reveals The Laws Of The Universe. It explains the Law of the Seed, the Law of the Harvest, the Law of Love, the Law of Process and the Law of Eventuality, and even the Law of Truth. "The Law of Truth was in his mouth" (Malachi 2:6; see also Ezekiel 44:4,5).

5. The Word Of God Is A Relationship Handbook. It reveals how to maintain worthy relationships. It exposes fools and how to recognize those who do not qualify for relationship.

6. The Word Of God Is A Worship Encyclopedia. "God is a Spirit: and they that worship Him must worship Him in Spirit and in truth" (John 4:24). The Word of God explains worship and its value and importance in your daily life. God inhabits the praises of His people. So, the Word of God shows you how to conduct yourself in His presence and how to attract His presence (read Psalm 100:2).

7. The Word Of God Teaches Spiritual Protocol. It reveals the appropriate conduct necessary in...

▶ approaching *God* effectively;
▶ approaching *leaders* and those in authority;
▶ your relationship with your *parents and children.*

8. The Word Of God Is A Problem-Solving

Handbook. It reveals how to solve financial problems, sin problems, marriage problems and even how to solve church problems when strife arises.

9. The Word Of God Is A Deliverance Handbook For Captives. It contains the biography of Uncommon Deliverers of nations, of people and of the sick and afflicted. Gideon, Abraham, David, Paul and Jesus were Deliverers. The Word reveals how people become captives—and even explains the Assignment of every minister (read Isaiah 61:1).

10. The Word Of God Creates Conviction That Causes Change. Without conviction, you could live a lifetime in error and die without even moving toward God.

11. The Word Of God Is The Book Of Divine Secrets. "The *secret* of the Lord is with them that fear Him; and *He will shew them His covenant*" (Psalm 25:14; see also Genesis 18:17,18). It reveals the Secrets of Uncommon Achievers, the secrets of financial increase, victorious living and even uncommon promotion (see Proverbs 22:29).

Remember: *The Word Of God Is The Most Important Book On Earth.*

When You Change
Your *Focus*
You Will Change
Your *Feelings.*

-MIKE MURDOCK

∾ 2 ∾

THE WORD OF GOD CAN SOLVE EVERY PROBLEM IN YOUR LIFE.

The Word Is A Problem-Solving Manual.
Every solution necessary for your success is hidden in the powerful teachings of Christ and the remarkable biographies of Biblical champions.

12 Problems The Word Of God Can Solve In Your Life

1. The Word Of God Solves The Problem Of Depression. Jesus Himself stated, "These things have I spoken unto you, that My joy might remain in you, and that your joy might be full" (John 15:11).

In Nehemiah, when the people *understood* the law of God, they *rejoiced.* "...to make great mirth, because they had understood the words that were declared unto them" (Nehemiah 8:12).

2. The Word Of God Exposes Any Seeds Of Falsehood That Have Entered Your Life. "Thy Law is the Truth" (Psalm 119:142). "Thy Word is truth" (John 17:17).

3. The Word Of God Births The Fear Of God Within You. "And it shall be with him, and he shall read therein all the days of his life: that he may learn to fear the Lord his God, to keep all the words of this Law and these statutes, to do them" (Deuteronomy 17:19; see also Proverbs 1:1-5).

4. The Word Of God Destroys Sickness And Disease. "He sent His Word and healed them" (Psalm 107:20). "And said, If thou wilt diligently hearken to the Voice of the Lord thy God...and wilt give ear to His commandments, and keep all His statutes, I will put none of these diseases upon thee, which I have brought upon the Egyptians: for I am the Lord that healeth thee" (Exodus 15:26).

"...attend to My words;...for they are...health to all their flesh" (Proverbs 4:20,22).

5. The Word Of God Births Hope. "I have *hoped* in Thy Judgments" (Psalm 119:43).

"Remember the word unto Thy servant, upon which Thou hast caused me to hope" (Psalm 119:49,74).

6. The Word Of God Produces True Peace. "Oh that thou hadst hearkened to My commandments! Then had thy peace been as a river, and thy righteousness as the waves of the sea" (Isaiah 48:18). "I will hear what God the Lord will speak: for He will speak peace unto His people," (Psalm 85:8).

7. The Word Of God Solves Emotional Problems. "Great peace have they which love Thy Law: and *nothing shall offend them*" (Psalm 119:165). Emotional wounds occur through offenses. The Word of God is a shield and enables you to see the attacks of others as opportunities rather than obstacles.

8. The Word Of God Unleashes Uncommon Faith. Faith is confidence in God. Faith comes when the words of God enter your heart. "...faith cometh by hearing, and hearing by the Word of God" (Romans 10:17).

9. The Word Of God Enables You To Make Wise Decisions. "Keep sound wisdom...then shalt thou walk in thy way safely, and thy foot shalt not stumble" (Proverbs 3:21,23).

10. The Word Of God Solves Financial Problems. "Wherefore ye shall do My statutes...And the land shall yield her fruit, and ye shall eat your fill" (Leviticus 25:18,19).

Prosperity is always the result of obedience to a *Principle* of God. "If ye walk in My statutes, and keep My commandments, and do them; Then I will give you rain in due season, and the land shall yield her increase, and the trees of the field shall yield their fruit" (Leviticus 26:3,4).

"Blessed is the man that feareth the Lord, that delighteth greatly in His commandments...Wealth and riches shall be in his house" (Psalm 112:1,3).

11. The Word Of God Enables You To Withstand Temptation. "Thy Word have I hid in mine heart, that I might not sin against Thee" (Psalm 119:11; see also Luke 4:4, Matthew 4:4).

12. The Word Of God Increases Favor With God And Man. "Let not mercy and truth forsake thee: bind them about thy neck: write them upon the table of thine heart: So shalt thou find favour and good understanding in the sight of God and man" (Proverbs 3:3,4).

Your Passion for the Word of God is your greatest asset in your pursuit for success.

Remember: *The Word Of God Can Solve Every Problem In Your Life.*

Anything You Want!

"Your Word Is Changing Me!"©

Anything You want
Anything You ask
Whatever You desire
Just name the task
That's what I will do
That's what I will do
Precious Holy Spirit
I'm in love with You!

-MIKE MURDOCK

Love Songs to the Holy Spirit

❧ 3 ❧

THE HOLY SPIRIT USES THE WORD OF GOD AS THE INSTRUMENT FOR CHANGE IN YOUR LIFE.

Your Success Will Require Change.
That is why you need The Word of God.
The Bible is a Book about Change.
It provides *hope* for Change.
It imparts the *keys* to Change.
It provides *proof* people can Change.
It provides *examples* of those who succeeded in their Goals.

People Can Change. Saul, the tormenter, was *changed.* He became the Apostle Paul, the Mentor. He was changed through his encounter with God. When you read of this change, your faith will leap. The Word of God Paints a Portrait of Hope...for those around us who require change.

Without the Word of God, life can appear hopeless at times—when you are waiting for others to change, you need to have the inner confidence that God is involved. That is why the Bible is so important. It provides you with actual examples of such Changes.

Your Circumstances Can Change. The story of Joseph is a remarkable collection of miracles. Someone's anger can put you in the *pit*. Your faith in God can move you into the *palace*.

Your Finances Can Change. That's why The Word of God is so important. Read 1 Kings 17—slowly and aloud. The widow of Zarephath was impoverished. Her son was emaciated. They faced their last meal. But a man of God entered the picture. *When favor from God flows, a man of God with a Word of faith will step into your life.* The Word of God from a man of God corrects your focus.

Your Physical Condition Can Change. One woman had an issue of blood for 12 years. But The Word of God shows how her persistence to touch Christ brought *change*.

Your Life Can Change. "If any man be in Christ, he is a new creature: old things are passed away; behold, all things are become new" (2 Corinthians 5:17).

Your Sinful Nature Can Be Changed. "All have sinned" (Romans 3:23). The Word of God births conviction, repentance and transformation. "And be not conformed to this world: but be ye transformed by the renewing of your mind" (Romans 12:2).

The Word Of God Changes Your View Of Authority. Few enjoy submission to authority. But The Word guarantees God will honor us for it. "Let every soul be subject unto the higher powers. For there is no power but of God: the powers that be are ordained of God" (Romans 13:1).

The Word Of God Changes Your View Of Your Children. When your children break your heart, remember, "Children are an heritage of the

Lord: and the fruit of the womb is His reward" (Psalm 127:3).

The Word Of God Can Change Your View Toward Your Work. Work is a gift that births significance, recognition and financial provision for your family. "Every man also to whom God hath given riches and wealth, and hath given him power to eat thereof, and to take his portion, and to rejoice in his labour; this is the gift of God" (Ecclesiastes 5:19; see also 1 Timothy 5:8).

The Word Of God Changes Your Focus. Introspection is deadly. Self-absorption destroys. The Word of God enables you to focus on the needs of others. "Knowing that whatsoever good thing any man doeth, the same shall he receive of the Lord, whether he be bond or free" (Ephesians 6:8). Your focus affects your faith.

When Job, in the midst of his adversity, focused on the needs of his friends, his circumstances changed. "And the Lord turned the captivity of Job, when he prayed for his friends: also the Lord gave Job twice as much as he had before" (Job 42:10).

The Word Of God Shows Examples Of Those Who Are Unwilling To Change. Jezebel would not change, and God removed her. Ahab refused to change, and he died in his sins. Korah refused to change, and his entire family suffered the consequences. The cry of Jesus to Israel was to change. "How often would I have gathered thy children together, even as a hen gathereth her chickens under her wings, and ye would not!" (Matthew 23:37).

Remember: *The Holy Spirit Uses The Word Of God As The Instrument For Change In Your Life.*

The Waves Of
    Yesterday's Disobedience
Always Splash On
    The Shores Of Today.

-MIKE MURDOCK

≈ 4 ≈

YOUR OBEDIENCE TO THE WORD OF GOD WILL DETERMINE YOUR SUCCESS.

———➤-◦-◄———

Only The Obedient Are Guaranteed Rewards.

God has never responded to Needs. The world is still filled with millions of people who are needy, hopeless and desperate for help.

God has never responded to Pain. Millions live in daily pain—financial, physical and mental, and yet never experience change.

God has always responded to Obedience. Obedience alone attracts God.

God's Only *Pleasure* Is To Be *Believed.*

God's Only *Pain* Is To Be *Doubted.*

One Bible verse reveals the essence of God, "God is not a man, that He should lie; neither the son of man, that He should repent: hath He said, and shall He not do it? or hath He spoken, and shall He not make it good?" (Numbers 23:19).

God is only pleasured when His Word is believed. "But without faith it is impossible to please Him: for he that cometh to God must believe that He is, and that He is a rewarder of them that diligently seek Him" (Hebrews 11:6; see also Proverbs 4:20,21).

Your *knowledge* of the Word of God—does not guarantee your success. *Your obedience to The Word of God determines your success* (see James 2:21-23).

1. Your Success On Your Job Is Affected By The Word Of God. The Bible reveals what elevates men. "Seest thou a man diligent in his business? he shall stand before kings; he shall not stand before mean men" (Proverbs 22:29).

2. Your Success In Your Family Life Is Affected By Your Obedience To The Word Of God.

Your success with your children. "And, ye fathers, provoke not your children to wrath: but bring them up in the nurture and admonition of the Lord" (Ephesians 6:4).

Your success with your mate. "So ought men to love their wives as their own bodies. He that loveth his wife loveth himself. For no man ever yet hated his own flesh; but nourisheth and cherisheth it, even as the Lord the church:" (Ephesians 5:28,29).

"For after this manner in the old time the holy women also, who trusted in God, adorned themselves, being in subjection unto their own husbands:" (1 Peter 3:5).

3. Your Financial Success Is Affected By Your Obedience To The Word Of God. "Blessed is the man... that delighteth greatly in His commandments. Wealth and riches shall be in his house: and his righteousness endureth for ever" (Psalm 112:1,3).

Remember: *Your Obedience To The Word Of God Will Determine Your Success In Life.*

❧ 5 ❧

YOUR IGNORANCE OF THE WORD OF GOD IS THE ONLY EFFECTIVE WEAPON AN ENEMY CAN USE AGAINST YOU.

Ignorance Is Deadly.

Scripture proves it. "My people are destroyed for lack of knowledge" (Hosea 4:6).

Not demons.

Not enemies.

Destruction can only occur to the ignorant.

God is a God of knowledge and Wisdom. "And the Spirit of the Lord shall rest upon Him, the Spirit of Wisdom...the Spirit of Knowledge" (Isaiah 11:2; see also Ephesians 1:17).

A remarkable photograph of Jesus is provided for us in Matthew 4. He is on a fast. His body is weakened. There, alone, without the encouragement of a multitude cheering Him, satan approached Him. Taunting, tempting and appealing to His natural senses. What was the response of Jesus? Simple. But, effective, "It is *written.*"

Jesus *knew* the Word.

Jesus *spoke* the Word.

Jesus *is* the Word!

When Leaders become obsessed with the Word of God, they will birth people obsessed with the Word of God.

When Leaders *speak* the Word, the people will *live* the Word.

The *Price* of His presence is *Time*.

The *Purpose* of His presence is *Change*.

The *Product* of His presence is *Holiness*.

The goal of satan is Ignorance.

It is his *only* weapon.

Satan does not fear your sinning. God will forgive.

Satan does not fear your depression. God will enter and drive it away.

Satan does not fear your poverty. God will provide.

Satan fears your discovery of The Word of God. He is helpless against your knowledge of God.

Remember: *Your Ignorance Of The Word Of God Is The Only Effective Weapon An Enemy Can Use Against You.*

≈ 6 ≈

Your Reaction To The Word Of God Determines The Reaction Of God Toward You And Your Family.

Your Opinion Of The Word Is Contagious.

Your children will be affected by your respect for The Word of God. "Seeing thou hast forgotten the Law of thy God, I will also forget thy children" (Hosea 4:6).

Your Reaction To The Word Of God Determines God's Reaction To Your Children. It takes much more than religious ritual to impress God.

Humans judge the love of others by *words* spoken. I have heard it countless times...

"My father never *told* me he loved me."

"My husband rarely *tells* me he loves me."

"My childhood was lacking in *affection*."

Those speaking these words admitted that their father paid the bills, provided a home and was good to them. But, they were upset because he never—

spoke his love.

God had a *different* viewpoint. "This people draweth nigh unto Me with their mouth, and honoureth Me with their lips; but their heart is far from Me" (Matthew 15:8).

Words alone do not impress God.

Obedience impresses God. "If ye abide in Me, and My Words abide in you, ye shall ask what ye will, and it shall be done unto you" (John 15:7).

4 Steps To Building A Spiritual Home

1. Select A Plan To Familiarize Your Family With The Word Of God. Here is an example:

The Topical Plan. Choose a Topic. Every day for 31 consecutive days...read the Scriptures about that Topic at breakfast. Example: The Topic of faith.

▶ Use *examples* of faith (the blind man crying out to Jesus for his healing).

▶ Show *examples* of those who did *not* have faith, such as the ten spies who returned from Canaan with an "evil report."

▶ Read aloud to your family about the *Heroes of Faith*, in Hebrews 11.

▶ Explain the *necessity* of faith. "Without faith, it is impossible to please Him" (Hebrews 11:6).

2. Memorize One Scripture Each Morning. It sounds simple. But, few will. Do you realize that within 12 months, you could quote freely 365 Scriptures...memorizing just one simple verse a day? *Write it* on a piece of paper or card. *Keep it* in your pocket. *Refer to it* throughout the day. *Place it* on the dashboard of your car. Make a tent card, on top of your TV or desk.

3. Select A Specific Place To Read The Word Of God Daily. It may be in your recliner, in the corner of your bedroom or at the breakfast table each morning.

Attach this habit to an existing habit. For instance, one man ate breakfast every morning, same time, every day. So, he kept his Bible next to his plate and read it *before* his breakfast every day. He understood building a habit...on an *existing* habit.

4. Keep Your Daily Scripture Next To Your Telephone. Every day you talk to friends and business associates. *Viewing that* Scripture while you are discussing matters with them will remind you to *speak* The Word of God, *impart* The Word of God and *encourage them* through The Word of God.

One morning, I came out of The Secret Place at my home to get a glass of water. The phone rang. I thought, "Why not?"

It was a minister friend. He was in trouble. As we talked, my heart ached to get back into *The Secret Place.* He talked, wept and I listened. Then suddenly, it dawned on me. This was the purpose of *The Secret Place!* To equip me to impart to him during this time.

I turned the telephone call into a prayer meeting. As I prayed The *Word*, victory emerged. I heard joy spring up from his heart. I turned the telephone conversation into Seed-time for sowing The Word of God and prayer.

Build Word consciousness into your family.

Place Scripture plaques on your walls.

Have Scriptures on your napkins.

Have Scriptures on your pencils.

Climatize your home with the Word of God...everywhere.

The first 47 CD's in my CD player...are Scripture CD's reading the Bible from Genesis 1 through Revelation 22.

I wrote this song one day in my Secret Place:

> Thy Word is all that matters.
> Thy Word is all that matters.
> Thy Word is all that matters.
> Thy Word, *Thy Holy Word!*

Remember: *Your Reaction To The Word Of God Determines God's Reaction To Your Family.*

❧ 7 ❧

THE MOST VALUABLE SUCCESS HABIT IN YOUR LIFE IS YOUR DAILY READING OF THE WORD OF GOD.

Your Habits Are Deciding Your Future.

Habit is a good word. It simply means that anything you do twice...becomes *easier.* Many people confuse discipline and habit.

Discipline is a conscious effort to birth a habit.

Habit is unconscious behavior requiring no effort.

Psychologists tell us that anything you do for 30 consecutive days, will become a habit.

The Bible is full of examples of those who had certain habits. David prayed seven times a day. Daniel prayed three times a day. Jesus said, "I sat *daily* with you teaching in the temple" (Matthew 26:55).

So, your success depends on *habits* that move you toward your desired goals and dreams.

Many years ago, a very successful business woman in Dallas, Texas, had the simple habit of planning each day. She wrote six tasks down on a sheet of paper each morning. She chose only the six most important tasks that deserved her total attention. She worked on them in the order of their priority. At her death, she was worth a fortune...and much of her success was attributed to this simple *daily habit.*

One of the great preachers of America has a simple, but effective, morning habit. Each morning, he enters his prayer time at 5:30 to 6:30. One hour a day provides him remarkable insight, courage and strength. *One simple daily habit.*

Successful People Do *Daily* What Unsuccessful People Do *Occasionally.*

If you fail with your life, you will be able to trace your failure to something that you permitted to occur daily—in your mind, home or life.

If you succeed with your life, anyone studying your success will find a major influence was in something you have done each day.

I urge you to focus on birthing a daily success habit—The Word of God. If you will build your entire day around this simple habit, you will change your attitude, energy and Wisdom...*forever.*

4 Personal Bible Reading Secrets

1. Find The Bible You Love To Read. It may be large print and even difficult to carry. Keep this Bible in your Secret Place daily. Mark the passages that inspire you. I use the following marking colors in my personal Bible:

Red...for my *passion*, the Holy Spirit.

Blue...for my *Assignment*, any Wisdom Scriptures concerning The Word of God.

Green...for *prosperity* promised for my obedience.

Yellow...for *Memory Scriptures* engraved in the heart.

2. Decide The Bible You Love To Carry. Usually, these are small Bibles difficult to read. But, your focus is to keep conscious of His Word...every moment.

3. Start With An Achievable Goal. Begin each morning with one chapter a day. One of the best systems I ever utilized was reading the book of Proverbs. It contains 31 chapters. On the first day of each month, read chapter 1. On day two, read chapter 2. As you continue reading a chapter a day, something will grow inside you. Setting an *achievable* goal like this will build your confidence, your consciousness of God and even change your portrait of yourself. Later, you can choose a greater goal.

4. Link This New Bible Habit To An Existing Habit...Something You Are Already Doing. For example, for many years, I read the Bible the first thing each morning...by kneeling beside my bed immediately upon arising. Others read it at the breakfast table...*faithfully*.

9 Wisdom Keys To Remember As You Birth The Success Habit Of Reading The Word Of God Daily

1. When You Enter The Presence Of God, Your *Weakness* Will Die.

2. When The Wisdom Of God Enters Your Heart, Your *Decisions* Will Change.

3. Men Do Not Decide Their Future, They

Decide Their *Habits* And Their Habits Then Create Their *Future.*

4. **Something You Are Doing *Daily* Will Decide Your Future Success Or Tragedy.**

5. **Successful People Do *Daily* What Unsuccessful People Do *Occasionally.***

6. **One Hour In The Presence Of God Can Reveal The Fatal Flaws Of Your Most Carefully Laid Plans.**

7. **When The Word Of God Enters Your Heart, Your *Faith In God* Will Increase.**

8. **When The Word Of God Is Sown Into Your *Mind*, Your Mouth Will Begin To Speak His Words.**

9. **When You Speak The Word Of God, The *Miracles Of God* Will Occur In Your Life.**

Remember: *The Most Valuable Success Habit In Your Life Is Your Daily Reading Of The Word Of God.*

Our Prayer Together...

"Holy Spirit, thank You today for Your holy and precious Word. Without it, we would fail. You have chosen to provide an invaluable Weapon to defeat every foe— Your Holy Word.

"Thank You for the example of Jesus, Who used The Word to withstand the tempter in the greatest crisis of His life.

"Today, Birth a new passion this very moment for Your Word. Today, reveal to me now how important Your Word is to my survival and my success. Today, I expect my new focus and passion on Your Word to change my heart, my circumstances and my decision making...*forever.*

"In the Name of Jesus, I receive a new anointing

and new passion for The Word of God now. Amen."

My Closing Thought

If this Wisdom Book has blessed you, I'd love to hear from you! You may order additional copies for a friend, cell group, or associates at your workplace. *The Greatest Gift Of All...Is The Gift Of Wisdom.*

——————— Quantity Price List For ———————
Seeds Of Wisdom On The Word Of God (B-117)

QUANTITY	COST EACH	DISCOUNT	QUANTITY	COST EACH	DISCOUNT
1-9	= $5.00 ea.	Retail	2000-4999	= $2.00 ea.	60%
10-499	= $3.00 ea.	40%	5000-up	= Contact Office	
500-1999	= $2.50 ea.	50%			

(Add 10% shipping single titles only.)

READING THE BIBLE THROUGH IN ONE MONTH

1. Gen. 1-40
2. Gen. 41-50 / Ex. 1-30
3. Ex. 31-40 / Lev. 1-27 / Num. 1-3
4. Num. 4-36 / Deut. 1-7
5. Deut. 8-34 / Josh. 1-13
6. Josh. 14-24 / Jud. 1-21 / Ruth 1-4 / 1 Sam. 1-4
7. 1 Sam. 5-31 / 2 Sam. 1-13
8. 2 Sam. 14-24 / 1 Ki. 1-22 / 2 Ki. 1-7
9. 2 Ki. 8-25 / 1 Chron. 1-22
10. 1 Chron. 23-29 / 2 Chron. 1-33
11. 2 Chron. 34-36 / Ezra 1-10 / Neh. 1-13 / Esth. 1-10 / Job 1-4
12. Job 5-42 / Ps. 1-2
13. Ps. 3-42
14. Ps. 43-82
15. Ps. 83-122
16. Ps. 123-150 / Prov. 1-12
17. Prov. 13-31 / Eccl. 1-12 / Song 1-8 / Isa. 1
18. Isa. 2-41
19. Isa. 42-66 / Jer. 1-15
20. Jer. 16-52 / Lam. 1-3
21. Lam. 4-5 / Ez. 1-40
22. Ez. 41-48 / Dan. 1-12 / Hos. 1-14 / Joel 1-3 / Amos 1-3
23. Amos 4-9 / Obadiah 1 / Jonah 1-4 / Micah 1-7 / Nahum 1-3 / Hab. 1-3 / Zeph. 1-3 / Hag. 1-2 / Zech. 1-14 / Mal. 1-4
24. Matt. 1-28 / Mark 1-12
25. Mark 13-16 / Luke 1-24 / John 1-12
26. John 13-21 / Acts 1-28 / Rom. 1-3
27. Rom. 4-16 / 1 Cor. 1-16 / 2 Cor. 1-11
28. 2 Cor. 12-13 / Gal. 1-6 / Eph. 1-6 / Phil. 1-4 / Col. 1-4 / 1 Thes. 1-5 / 2 Thes. 1-3 / 1 Tim. 1-6 / 2 Tim. 1-4
29. Titus 1-3 / Philemon 1 / Heb. 1-13 / James 1-5 / 1 Pet. 1-5 / 2 Pet. 1-3 / 1 John 1-5 / 2 John 1 / 3 John 1 / Jude 1
30. Rev. 1-22

DECISION

DR. MIKE MURDOCK

Will You Accept Jesus As Your Personal Savior Today?

The Bible says, "That if thou shalt confess with thy mouth the Lord Jesus, and shalt believe in thine heart that God hath raised Him from the dead, thou shalt be saved" (Romans 10:9).

Pray this prayer from your heart today!

"Dear Jesus, I believe that You died for me and rose again on the third day. I confess I am a sinner...I need Your love and forgiveness... Come into my heart. Forgive my sins. I receive Your eternal life. Confirm Your love by giving me peace, joy and supernatural love for others. Amen."

is in tremendous demand as one of the most dynamic speakers in America today.

More than 14,000 audiences in 38 countries have attended his meetings and seminars. Hundreds of invitations come to him from churches, colleges and business corporations. He is a noted author of over 140 books, including the best sellers, *"The Leadership Secrets of Jesus"* and *"Secrets of the Richest Man Who Ever Lived."* Thousands view his weekly television program, *"Wisdom Keys with Mike Murdock."* Many attend his Schools of Wisdom that he hosts in major cities of America.

☐ Yes, Mike! I made a decision to accept Christ as my personal Savior today. Please send me my free gift of your book, *"31 Keys to a New Beginning"* to help me with my new life in Christ. *(B-48)*

NAME   BIRTHDAY

ADDRESS

CITY   STATE   ZIP

PHONE   E-MAIL

Mail form to:
The Wisdom Center • 4051 Denton Hwy. •Ft. Worth, TX 76117
Phone: 1-888-WISDOM-1 (1-888-947-3661)
Website: ***thewisdomcenter.tv***

Recommended Books And Tapes:

Wisdom Key Booklet: "Greatest Success Habit On Earth" *(B-80 / $3)*

"One-Minute Pocket Bible For Fathers" *(B-51 / $5)*

"One-Minute Pocket Bible For Mothers" *(B-52 / $5)*

"Wisdom Keys from Every Book," Vol. 1, Genesis-Joshua, 6-Tape Series *(TS-41 / $30)*

"Wisdom Keys from Every Book," Vol. 2, Judges-2 Kings, 6-Tape Series *(TS-42 / $30)*

"Wisdom Keys from Every Book," Vol. 3, 1 Chr.-Job, 6-Tape Series *(TS-43 / $30)*

"The Blessing Bible" *(B-28 / $10)*

THE WISDOM CENTER
4051 DENTON HWY.
FT. WORTH, TX 76117
1-888-WISDOM-1
(1-888-947-3661)
Website:
thewisdomcenter.tv

Dear Friend,

You matter. You are important to God. If you need special prayer, don't hesitate to write me today.

My staff and I will pray for you. I will write you back.

God has brought us together for a reason.

Will you become my Monthly Faith Partner?

Your Seeds of Loving Support will bless so many...and birth uncommon increase in your own life.

When you sow, expect Four Scriptural Harvests:

▶ Uncommon Protection (Malachi 3:10,11)
▶ Uncommon Favor (Luke 6:38)
▶ Uncommon Health (Isaiah 58:8)
▶ Uncommon Financial Ideas (Deuteronomy 8:18)

An Uncommon Seed Always Creates An Uncommon Harvest (Mark 10:28-30).

Looking for your letter,

Mike Murdock

THE WISDOM CENTER

1-888-WISDOM-1 (1-888-947-3661)

Mon.-Fri.
8 AM-5 PM CST

visit us at:
www.thewisdomcenter.cc

PRODUCT NUMBER	PRODUCT DESCRIPTION	QTY	PRICE	TOTAL
				1
				2
				3
				4
				5
				6

SubTotal		$ 7
Canada ADD 20%		$ 8
S/H Add 10%		$ 9
TOTAL		$ 10
My Seed Offering		$ 11

Your Seed Faith Offering is used to support the MIKE MURDOCK Evangelistic Association, The Wisdom Center, and all its programs. Applicable law requires that we have the discretion to allocate donations in order to carry out our charitable purpose. In the event MMEA receives more funds for the project than needed, excess funds will be used for another worthy outreach.

DISCOUNTS
Bookstore/Distributors

QTY.	DISCOUNT	
1-9	Retail	
10-499	40%	
500-1999	50%	
2000-4999	60%	
5000 & Up	Contact Office	

(single titles only)

Name _____

Address _____

City _____ State _____ Zip _____

Phone _____ Email _____

Method of Payment
☐ Cash ☐ Check ☐ Visa ☐ Mc ☐ Amex ☐ Discover

Card# _____

Birthday [MO] [DAY]   Expiration Date [ ][ ][ ][ ]

Total Enclosed $ _____ Signature _____

(Sorry No C.O.D.'s)

B-117

My Dear Friend,

Your success is determined by your love for the Word of God.

The most important success habit in life is reading and understanding the Wisdom of God...through the Holy Scriptures. The Word of God is your Wisdom for Life (Deut. 4:6). The only weapon satan can effectively use against you is your ignorance of the Word (Hosea 4:6).

That's why I wrote this book...just for you.

When I pray for you in The Secret Place, I am asking God to unleash the strongest passion you've ever experienced...to know Him through His Word. It will change your focus, health, financial freedom and especially your inner peace.

Your Seeds are scheduling a Divine Harvest. The Seeds That Leave Your Hand Never Leave Your Life—They Simply Go Into Your Future Where They Multiply.

Wrap your faith around your Seed this week. Focus it for a desired result. Expect a 100-fold return. Jesus promised it! (Mark 10:28-30). Expect uncommon health and healing, uncommon protection and uncommon peace as part of the promise.

Use the envelope inside this book when you write me back. Your letter is the lifeline of this ministry.

Your Prayer Partner,

Mike Murdock

SCHOOL of WISDOM #2

VOLUME 2

The
SCHOOL
of
WISDOM
on

101
WISDOM KEYS
THAT HAVE
MOST CHANGED
MY LIFE

MIKE MURDOCK

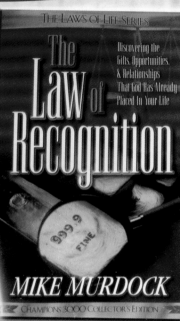

THE LAWS OF LIFE SERIES

The
Law of
Recognition

Discovering the
Gifts, Opportunities,
& Relationships
That God Has Already
Placed In Your Life

999.9 FINE

MIKE MURDOCK

CHAMPIONS 3000 COLLECTOR'S EDITION

DR. MIKE MURDOCK
P.O. BOX 99 • DALLAS, TEXAS • 75221

The School of Wisdom

▸ 47 Keys In Recognizing The Mate God Has Approved For You

▸ 14 Facts You Should Know About Your Gifts and Talents

▸ 17 Important Facts You Should Remember About Your Weakness

▸ And Much, Much More...

▸ What Attracts Others Toward You

▸ The Secret Of Multiplying Your Financial Blessings

▸ What Stops The Flow Of Your Faith

▸ Why Some Fail And Others Succeed

▸ How To Discern Your Life Assignment

▸ How To Create Currents Of Favor With Others

▸ How To Defeat Loneliness

 THE WISDOM CENTER
4051 Denton Highway • Fort Worth, TX 76117

1-888-WISDOM1
(1-888-947-3661)

Website:
THEWISDOMCENTER.TV

A

THE *Power* 7

VOLUME 13 — SEEDS of WISDOM on the SECRET PLACE — MIKE MURDOCK

VOLUME 14 — SEEDS of WISDOM on the HOLY SPIRIT — MIKE MURDOCK

VOLUME 20 — SEEDS of WISDOM on YOUR ASSIGNMENT — MIKE MURDOCK

VOLUME 25 — SEEDS of WISDOM on GOAL SETTING — MIKE MURDOCK

MY PERSONAL DREAM BOOK — The Mike Murdock School of Wisdom Series

101 WISDOM KEYS — Mike Murdock

31 Keys To A New Beginning

The Power 7 Pak

► Seeds of Wisdom on The Secret Place (B-115 / $5)
► Seeds of Wisdom on The Holy Spirit (B-116 / $5)
► Seeds of Wisdom on Your Assignment (B-122 / $5)
► Seeds of Wisdom on Goal Setting (B-127 / $5)
► My Personal Dream Book (B-143 / $5)
► 101 Wisdom Keys (B-45 / $5)
► 31 Keys To A New Beginning (B-48 / $5)

The Wisdom Center

**All 7 Books
Only $20**
WBL-19

Wisdom Is The Principal Thing

Add 10% For S/H

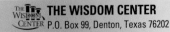

B | THE WISDOM CENTER
P.O. Box 99, Denton, Texas 76202

1-888-WISDOM1
(1-888-947-3661)

Website:
WWW.THEWISDOMCENTER.TV

Financial Success.

31 REASONS PEOPLE DO NOT RECEIVE THEIR FINANCIAL HARVEST

7 KEYS to 1000 TIMES MORE

The Lord God Of Your Fathers Make You A Thousand Times So Many More As You Are, And Bless You, As He Hath Promised You! *Deuteronomy 1:11*

MIKE MURDOCK

▶ 8 Scriptural Reasons You Should Pursue Financial Prosperity

▶ The Secret Prayer Key You Need When Making A Financial Request To God

▶ The Weapon Of Expectation And The 5 Miracles It Unlocks

▶ How To Discern Those Who Qualify To Receive Your Financial Assistance

▶ How To Predict The Miracle Moment God Will Schedule Your Financial Breakthrough

▶ Habits Of Uncommon Achievers

▶ The Greatest Success Law I Ever Discovered

▶ How To Discern Your Place Of Assignment, The Only Place Financial Provision Is Guaranteed

▶ 3 Secret Keys In Solving Problems For Others

The Wisdom Center

Video Pak AMVIDEO **$30**
Buy 1-Get 1 Free
(A $60 Value!)

Wisdom Is The Principal Thing

Add 10% For S/H

THE WISDOM CENTER
4051 Denton Highway • Fort Worth, TX 76117

1-888-WISDOM1
(1-888-947-3661)

Website:
THEWISDOMCENTER.TV

C

Songs From The Secret Place

The Music Ministry of MIKE MURDOCK

Love Songs To The Holy Spirit
Birthed In The Secret Place

THE HOLY SPIRIT HANDBOOK

What You Need To Know About Your Daily Companion, The Holy Spirit

Volume 1

MIKE MURDOCK

Songs...

1. A Holy Place
2. Anything You Want
3. Everything Comes From You
4. Fill This Place With Your Presence
5. First Thing Every Morning
6. Holy Spirit, I Want To Hear You
7. Holy Spirit, Move Again
8. Holy Spirit, You Are Enough
9. I Don't Know What I Would Do Without You
10. I Let Go (Of Anything That Stops Me)
11. I'll Just Fall On You
12. I Love You, Holy Spirit
13. I'm Building My Life Around You
14. I'm Giving Myself To You
15. I'm In Love! I'm In Love!
16. I Need Water (Holy Spirit, You're My Well)
17. In The Secret Place
18. In Your Presence, I'm Always Changed
19. In Your Presence (Miracles Are Born)
20. I've Got To Live In Your Presence
21. I Want To Hear Your Voice
22. I Will Do Things Your Way
23. Just One Day At A Time
24. Meet Me In The Secret Place
25. More Than Ever Before
26. Nobody Else Does What You Do
27. No No Walls!
28. Nothing Else Matters Anymore (Since I've Been In The Presence Of You Lord)
29. Nowhere Else
30. Once Again You've Answered
31. Only A Fool Would Try (To Live Without You)
32. Take Me Now
33. Teach Me How To Please You
34. There's No Place I'd Rather Be
35. Thy Word Is All That Matters
36. When I Get In Your Presence
37. You're The Best Thing (That's Ever Happened To Me)
38. You Are Wonderful
39. You've Done It Once
40. You Keep Changing Me
41. You Satisfy

Add 10% For S/H

The Uncommon Woman

MIKE MURDOCK

THE WISDOM FOR WOMEN SERIES

THIRTY - ONE SECRETS of an UNFORGETTABLE WOMAN

Master Secrets from the Life of Ruth

▸ **Master Keys In Understanding The Man In Your Life**

▸ **The One Thing Every Man Attempts To Move Away From**

▸ **The Dominant Difference Between A Wrong Woman And A Right Woman**

▸ **What Causes Men To Withdraw**

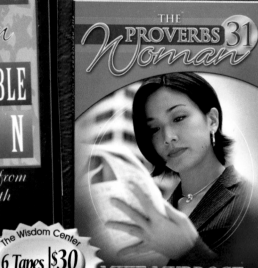

THE PROVERBS 31 Woman

MIKE MURDOCK

MENTORSHIP PROGRAM OF WISDOM

THE WISDOM CENTER
THE WISDOM CENTER
MIKE MURDOCK•P.O. Box 99• Denton, Texas

31 Secrets of an Unforgettable Woman

The Wisdom Center
6 Tapes | **$30**
PAK-009
Wisdom Is The Principal Thing

Free Book Enclosed!
Wisdom Is The Principal Thing

 THE WISDOM CENTER
4051 Denton Highway • Fort Worth, TX 76117

1-888-WISDOM1
(1-888-947-3661)

Website:
THEWISDOMCENTER.TV

E

UNCOMMON WISDOM FOR
AN UNCOMMON MINISTRY

FOR Ministers ONLY

THE UNCOMMON MINISTER
Power Principles For Hitting Your Target For Success In Ministry
1
MIKE MURDOCK

THE UNCOMMON MINISTER
Wisdom Keys For A Ministry Of Excellence And Greatness
2
MIKE MURDOCK

THE UNCOMMON MINISTER
Winning Principles For Achieving Greatness In Your Ministry
3

THE UNCOMMON MINISTER
Principles On The Path To A Victorious Ministry
4
MURDOCK

THE UNCOMMON MINISTER
Sign Posts On The Road To Excellence In Ministry
5
MIKE MURDOCK

THE UNCOMMON MINISTER
Powerful Steps To A More Powerful Ministry
6
MIKE MURDOCK

THE UNCOMMON MINISTER
Steps To Achieving Your Goals In Your Ministry
7
MIKE MURDOCK

Volume 1
Volume 2
Volume 3
Volume 4
Volume 5
Volume 6
Volume 7

The Wisdom Center
7 Books only $20
$35 value
PAKUM-1
Wisdom Is The Principal Thing

When God wants to touch a nation, He raises up a preacher. It is Uncommon Men and Women of God who have driven back the darkness and shielded the unlearned and rebellious from devastation by satanic forces. They offer the breath of life to a dead world. They open Golden Doors to Change. They unleash Forces of Truth in an age of deception.

An Uncommon Minister is prepared through seasons of pain, encounters with God, a mentors. Having sat at the feet of Uncommon Mentors his entire life, Dr. Mike Murdock shar practical but personal keys to increase the excellence and productivity of your ministry. Ea volume of "The Uncommon Minister" is handy, convenient and easy to read. Your load will lighter, your journey happier, and your effectiveness increased in "doing the will of the Father

Add 10% For S/H

GIFTS OF WISDOM...

FOR *Fathers* ONLY

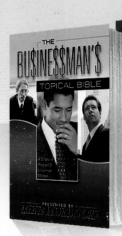

GIFTS OF WISDOM....

FOR *Mothers* ONLY!

Each Book Sold Separately

➤ **One-Minute Pocket Bible for Mothers** (B-52 / $5)

➤ **The Gift of Wisdom for Mothers** (B-70 / $10)

➤ **The Mother's Topical Bible** (B-36 / $10)

➤ **The Proverbs 31 Woman** (B-49 / $7)

➤ **The Uncommon Mother** (B-132 / $10)

➤ **Thirty-One Secrets of an Unforgettable Woman** (B-57 / $9)

The Wisdom Center

**WISDOM...
The Greatest
Gift Of All!**

Wisdom Is The Principal Thing

 THE WISDOM CENTER
4051 Denton Highway • Fort Worth, TX 76117

**1-888-WISDOM1
(1-888-947-3661)**

Website:
THEWISDOMCENTER.TV

I

GIFTS OF WISDOM...

SPECIALTY *Bibles*

*Each Book Sold Separately

My Gift Of Appreciation...
The Wisdom Commentary

The Wisdom Commentary includes
52 topics...for mentoring your
family every week of the year.

These topics include:

- Abilities
- Achievement
- Anointing
- Assignment
- Bitterness
- Blessing
- Career
- Change
- Children
- Dating
- Depression
- Discipline
- Divorce
- Dreams And Goals
- Enemy
- Enthusiasm
- Favor
- Finances
- Fools

- Giving
- Goal-Setting
- God
- Happiness
- Holy Spirit
- Ideas
- Intercession
- Jobs
- Loneliness
- Love
- Mentorship
- Ministers
- Miracles
- Mistakes
- Money
- Negotiation
- Prayer
- Problem-Solving
- Protégés

- Satan
- Secret Place
- Seed-Faith
- Self-Confidence
- Struggle
- Success
- Time-Management
- Understanding
- Victory
- Weaknesses
- Wisdom
- Word Of God
- Words
- Work

THE Mike Murdock COLLECTOR'S EDITION

The Wisdom Commentary of MIKE MURDOCK

THE WISDOM COMMENTARY 1

VOLUME 1

Gift Of Appreciation
For Your
Sponsorship
Seed of $100
or More
Gift Of Appreciation

My Gift Of Appreciation To My Sponsors!
Those Who Sponsor One Square Foot In
The Completion Of The Wisdom Center!

Thank you so much for becoming a part of this wonderful project...The completion of The Wisdom Center!
The total purchase and renovation cost of this facility (10,000 square feet) is just over $1,000,000. This is
approximately $100 per square foot. **The Wisdom Commentary is my Gift of Appreciation for your
Sponsorship Seed of $100...that sponsors one square foot of The Wisdom Center. Become a Sponsor!**
You will love this Volume 1, of The Wisdom Commentary. It is my exclusive Gift of Appreciation for The
Wisdom Key Family who partners with me in the Work of God as a Sponsor.

Add 10% For S/H

 THE WISDOM CENTER
4051 Denton Highway • Fort Worth, TX 76117

1-888-WISDOM1
(1-888-947-3661)

Website:
THEWISDOMCENTER.TV

K

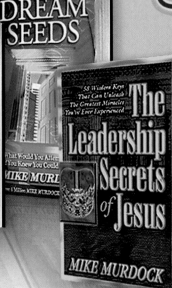
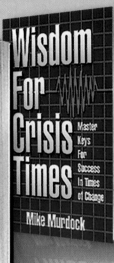

Master Secrets To Uncommon Increase.

7 KEYS to 1000 TIMES MORE

The Lord God Of Your Fathers Make You A Thousand Times So Many More As You Are, And Bless You, As He Hath Promised You!
Deuteronomy 1:11

MURDOCK

31 REASONS PEOPLE DO NOT RECEIVE THEIR FINANCIAL HARVEST

MIKE MURDOCK

THE WISDOM CENTER
MIKE MURDOCK • P.O. Box 99 • Denton, Texas

7 KEYS to 1000 TIMES MORE

The Wisdom Center
6 Tapes | $30
PAK-008
Wisdom Is The Principal Thing

The Wisdom Center
Free Book
B-82 ($12 Value)
Enclosed!
Wisdom Is The Principal Thing

The Greatest Success Law I Ever Discovered
Reasons God Wants To Increase Your Finances
3 Important Facts About Obedience

Add 10% For S/H

 THE WISDOM CENTER
4051 Denton Highway • Fort Worth, TX 76117

1-888-WISDOM1
(1-888-947-3661)

Website:
THEWISDOMCENTER.TV

M

The *Wisdom Journal*

"Write The Things Which Thou Hast Seen, And The Things Which Are, And The Things Which Shall Be Hereafter."

-Revelation 1:19

My Wisdom Journal

Stunningly beautiful deep Black and Gold Leatherette. Contains 160 pages for your personal journaling and diary...a different Wisdom Key for each day...it also includes:

► 101 Wisdom Keys

► 31 Facts About Favor

► 31 Facts About Wisdom

► 31 Facts About The Holy Spirit

► 31 Qualities Of An Unforgettable Woman

► 58 Leadership Secrets Of Jesus

► Read The Bible Through In A Year Program

► Sample Page For Effective Note Taking

The Wisdom Center

$20 Each

B-163

Wisdom Is The Principal Thing

Add 10% For S/H

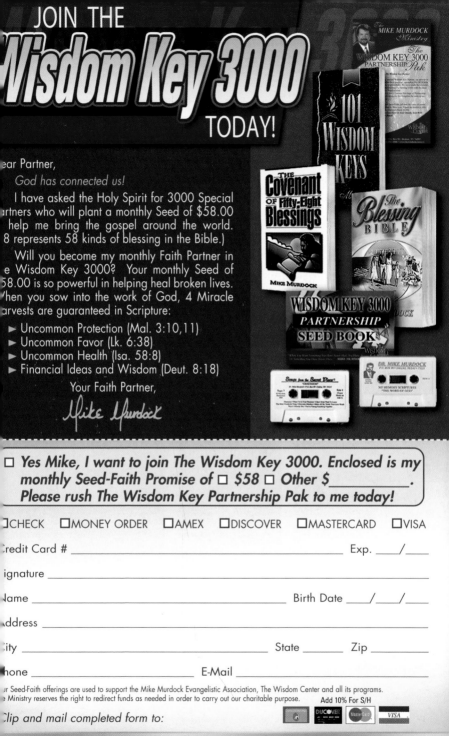